Calm for the Holidays

by

Rosemary Babikan

Volume 1 in a Series of Themed Mandalas

Happy Holidays!

To my family and friends

who have followed me along the many twists and turns

of my art journey, thank you for your support.

Whether you are a colorist,

or someone who appreciates the

patience and meticulous task of creating a mandala design,

this holiday book is for you.

Be calm and enjoy!

Introduction

Coloring a Mandala

The shape of the mandala is the universal symbol of a circle. It appears in all aspects of every day life ~ the solar system, weather, nature, art, architectural design, plant forms, and more. The circle illustrates wholeness, and represents the interconnectedness of all things. Drawing or coloring a mandala is a great tool for creating balance and relaxation. The circle pulls you into it, separating you from life's challenges outside the circle. Coloring repetitive patterns in a mandala requires stillness and focus while all other stresses of the day fall away. Your pulse rate goes down, your anxiety lessens, and your blood pressure relaxes, while the mind gives sole attention to the work. It rivals the practice of meditation and is easier for most people. This book is fun to color and perfect for gift giving during the holidays.

Designs are printed on only one side of the page. To make sure of no bleeding, slip a plain piece of paper behind the blank side.

This book belongs to

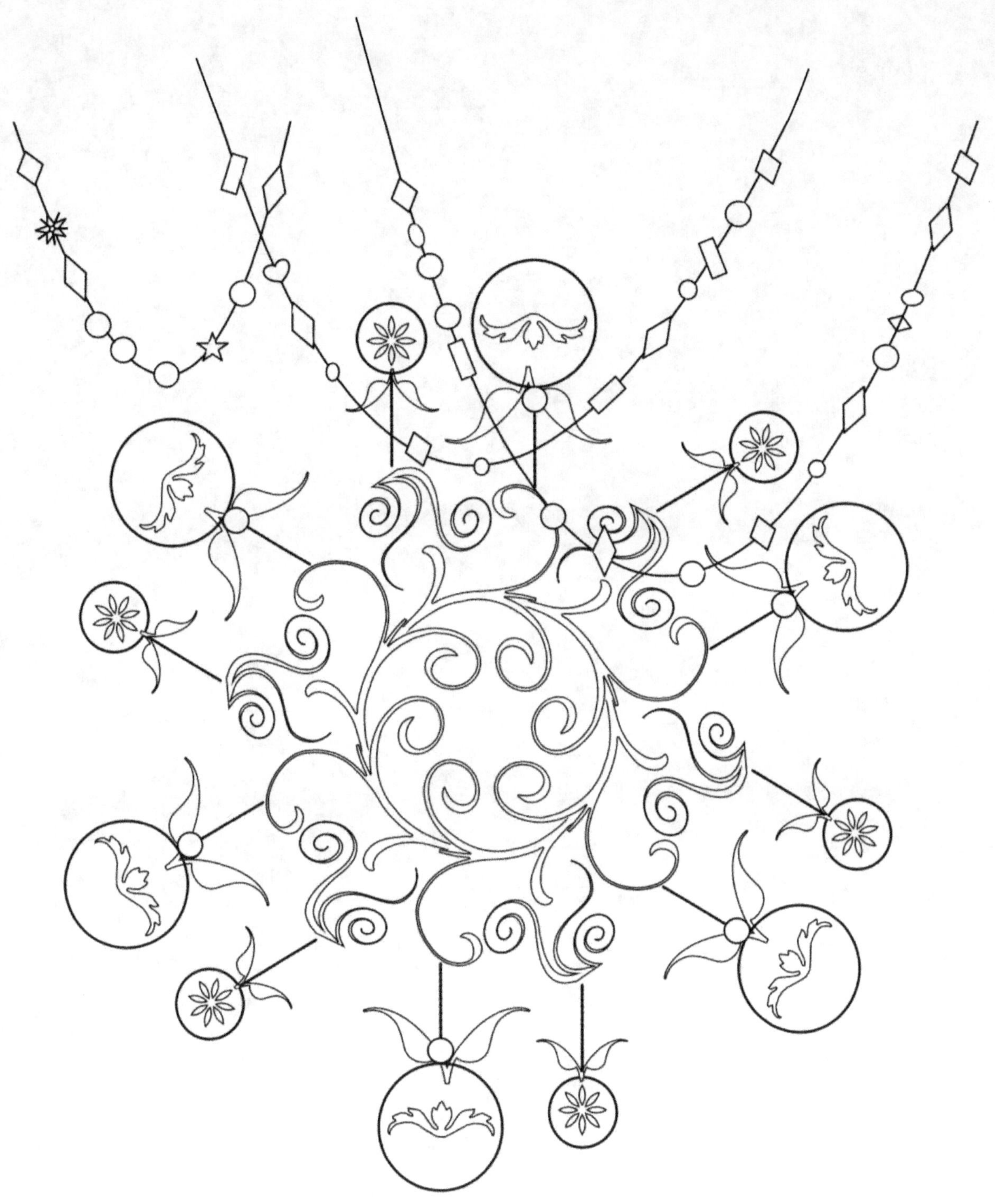

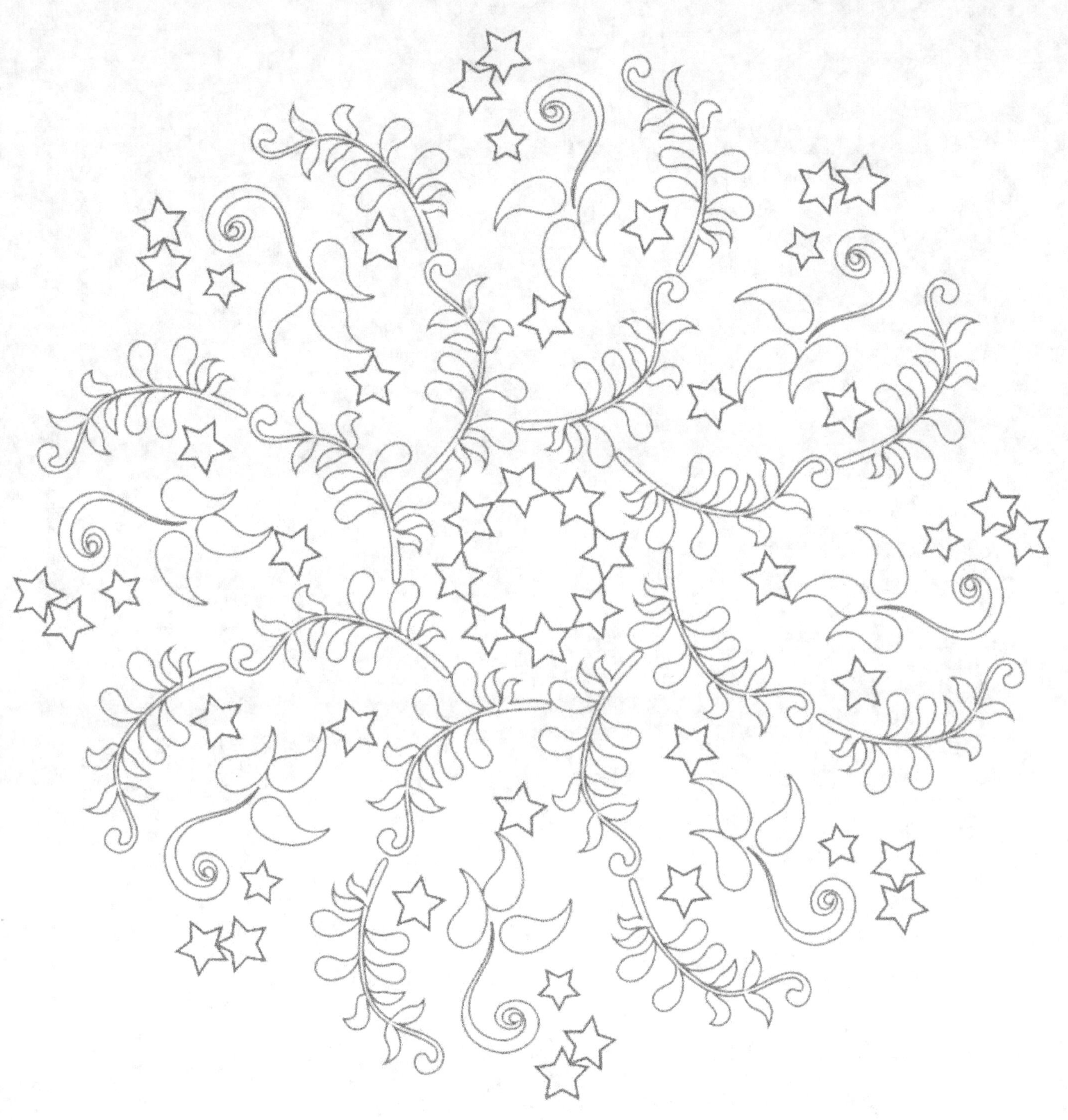

About the Author

Rosemary Babikan - illustration and coloring book artist.

She studied at the American Academy of Art in Chicago. Recently, she was bitten by the doodling bug, e.g., zentangling, adult coloring, and black and white ink drawings. After piling up hundreds of pieces of artwork, she decided to publish her own adult coloring book. The first one; *FairyTale Weddings, An Adult Coloring Book: An Enchanting Coloring Book*, was published in November of 2019. She followed that one with; Color Me Royal: Majestic Faces *and Magical Places,* in 2018. Currently, she is working on Volume 2 in a series of Themed Mandalas.
Besides reaping the benefits of a relaxing pastime, she gives you, the colorist, support to awaken your sleeping inner creativity. The structure of the picture is done, and the fun part begins for you. Calm for the Holidays is the first in her new mandala series, Themed Mandalas.

Look on Amazon and Barnes and Noble for:
 Fairytale Weddings, an Enchanting Coloring Book
 Color Me Royal, Majestic Faces and Magical Places
 rosemarybabikan.com ~ website

Coloring Hints for This Book

Coloring Snow ~ Is Snow Really White?

You've heard that out of the billions and billions
of snowflakes, not one is alike. Using infinite
shades of the spectrum to color snowflakes
will make them one-of-a-kind. A monotone color scheme -
different shades of one color - always works well giving
the snow dimension. An opposite color scheme makes your
pictures interesting with certain areas that will pop.
Lastly, a palette of colors in the same family can be a
challenge, but it makes your picture balanced and pleasing
to the eye. Never use black to darken a color. Use a few shades
darker, or the opposite color. Experiment and have fun!

Learning About the Color Spectrum

Primary Colors: Red, Blue, and Yellow

Secondary Colors: Orange, Green, and Purple

Monotone Colors: All shades of one color

Opposite Color Families ~ Reds and Greens, Blues and Oranges,
 Yellows and Purples

Same Family Palettes ~

Yellow:

Shades of Yellow, Yellow-Green, Green, Blue Green, and Blue

Blue:

Shades of Blue, Blue-Violet, Violet, Red-Violet, and Red

Red:

Shades of Red, Red-Orange, Orange, Orange-Yellow, Yellow

Practice Your Strokes and Shading

Practice Your Strokes and Shading

Testing Your Colors

Testing Your Colors